# The Tragedy in My Neighborhood

Also by Ken Cormier:

*Balance Act*

*First Printing*

ISBN-13: 978-0-615-35840-6
ISBN-10: 0615358403

Library of Congress Control Number: 2010923785

Cover Design Copyright © 2010 by Melissa Dickson Blackburn

# The Tragedy in My Neighborhood

Poems & Stories by Ken Cormier

*K C*

Dead Academics Press ~ HSEA Publishing ~ Opelika, AL ~ 2010

# Acknowledgments

Special thanks to Emily Cormier, Aaron Sanders, Scott Wilkerson, Jill Battson, Bob Holman, Penelope Pelizzon, Taylor Mali, Rich Martin, Patrick Penta, Jon Kleinman, Beth Bristow, Jean Cormier, Paul Cormier, Bobby Cormier, Matt Mayotte, Gale Dickau, John Ryan, Jason Courtmanche, Pamela Hayward, John Capecci, Lynn Bloom, Margaret Higonnet, Jon Andersen, Denise Abercrombie, Sean Forbes, Anne Hays, Laura Wetherington.

Grateful acknowledgment is made to the editors of the following journals in which some of the pieces in this collection appeared: *Storyscape, Toxic Poetry, textsound, 32 Poems, From the Fishouse, Euphony, Pasatiempo, THE Magazine,* and *Oddfellow Magazine.*

You can listen to Ken's audio productions of several of the poems and stories in this collection at www.kencormier.com/writing.

*This book is dedicated to*

*Aurore Cormier*

*(1913-2009)*

# Contents

# At the Poetry Reading

We quiet down to silence. The room quiets, except for a muffled snicker from the back. It's quiet in here now, deathly quiet in this room. The quietness of the room. Dead quiet. We can't imagine another room filled with a comparable number of people achieving this level of silence. We try to imagine in the quiet. We try, we keep trying. We try, and we think, yes. Yes, we've imagined it. We've imagined it now—a room filled with people, as quiet as this room. We imagined it, only for a moment, but imagine it we did. Briefly we managed to imagine the quietness of this room, as quiet as it is, measured against . . . replicated . . . happening . . . comparable . . . another, no. No, it doesn't seem possible. No, we haven't imagined another room as quiet as this. And now the host makes his announcements. He mentions poetry and we snicker and shift in our seats. He announces events and we guffaw and chortle. He eggs us on and we applaud, we erupt with applause. We shake the tables. We spill the coffee. We sip and clap. Sip tea, clap. We sip tea and shift in our seats. We wipe the spill. We shift. We shake the tables. The host sips the tea. He waits to egg us on. He straightens. He introduces the poet, the first poet of the evening. The poet. The poet is here. The poet, among us, is here and standing and meekly stepping forward. The poet is meek. The poet is stepping forward. The host eggs us on. We shake the tables. The meek poet steps forward. The poet embraces the host. (Secretly, the host eggs us on.) We shake the tables. We spill the coffee. The host recedes. We wipe the spill. We sip the tea, now in silence. We sip the tea, and the poet clears his throat. Clears his throat again, meekly. The meek poet gathers. He straightens his papers and gazes from beneath his tilted brow. We quiet down to silence, except for a snicker from the back of the room. The room quiets. The quietness of the room naturally precludes our imagining any other room, filled with a comparable number of people, as quiet as this. We quiet down. The poet, now gazing from beneath his tilted brow, begins to read aloud . . .

# We're Sitting on Buildings

*for Charles Mingus*

| | |
|---|---|
| We're sitting on buildings | Here! |
| We've got a big problem | Now! |
| Afraid of our nation | Oh! |
| But wanting to squeeze it | Through! |
| Went on an adventure | Then! |
| We found a new leader | Who! |
| Became like the others | Why! |
| Does that always happen | When! |
| We pray to Apollo | But! |
| We know nothing of him | So! |
| We wander with creatures | And! |
| Invade our own temples | Wake up! |
| | |
| Get out of the kitchen | Sink! |
| Climb under the counter | Which! |
| Was always your fortress | Bang! |
| We're tearing it down now | For! |
| Our children to see that | We! |
| Are nothing but monsters | Ha! |
| We season and flavor | Them! |
| To make them delicious | We! |
| Will strike and devour | Ow! |
| To choke on a backbone | It! |

11

| | |
|---|---|
| Is slowly reminding | Me! |
| To clean out the cupboard | Forget! |
| | |
| We're learning procedures | With! |
| A set of instructions | How! |
| Can we ever master | That! |
| Which always eludes us | Dogs! |
| Are biting my ankles | I! |
| Am fighting and kicking | My! |
| Most primitive moments | Have! |
| Been captured in movies | Still! |
| I am an enigma | Watch! |
| We can't help descending | Deep! |
| Into our own faces | Like! |
| Some kind of Narcissus | Relax! |

# My Work

My work has been translated into Polish and Chinese. My work carries a powerful incantatory vigor, the way Queequeg carries a full wheelbarrow on his back to Nantucket.

Achilles takes his bags Achilles takes his bags his bags Achilles takes his bags his bags and packs them in his heel.

My work has chased mercury across the bathroom floor, clapped hands and giggled with family, chased globules, metal shine. My work has pinched slippery globules, dividing, riding across the bathroom floor.

This next poem is for Plato. This next poem is for reporters, for Studs Terkel. This poem is for solutions that dissolve. This next poem is for believing that believing is not believing only. This next poem is for example. This poem is for

My work has been recorded on cassette tape, coughed into microphones. My work has been fed to things that *became*, has twice half-filled the attics and basements of my thrice-divorced mentors.

I never lived next door to Allen Ginsberg but ate sushi with him three years before he died. I never lived next door to never lived next. Allen Ginsberg's work has been published in Polish and

Chinese. My gentle tendril never untied inside. I never ate sushi with Allen Ginsberg three years after he died.

My work has walked through halls and strolled down malls and shopped in the shape of my old hometown. My work is a thick thesaurus used to boost and raise the full ashtrays in all my teachers' lounges. My work has been translated into Polish and Chinese.

# Albany

City of limitless joy, city where my anger treads,

loose-lipped and horse-hipped Albany,

a modicum of hair, a trench-mouthed, finger snapping

vision of gang fights in Albany, cheapskate

metaphors, debilitating back sores, accompanists sniffing ether,

completely stiffened,

camped out in socks and underwear, these first explorers, these

    several men

making their perilous journey so that someday Albany will abound,

this song is for you, Albany,

impressive Albany of the Old West,

stamped in oblivion, fictitious Albany,

Albany of my discontent,

thriving backwards Albany,

rinse-soaked Albany,

quietly rummaging through Albany,

Albany proper,

rancorous, deranged, ill-smelling Albany hung out

in rectories, worshiping false gods in Albany,

complying with draconian rules in Albany, irritating old sores,

cold sores in Albany, hopping from bar to bar, suffering

backbone, replete with nonsense, keepsake Albany, snow globe

    Albany,

oft forgotten, never forgiven,

my dear old Albany.

# The Sounds of Lunch

I'm able to spend more time writing music now. I quit my job. I have more time now to relax. I wake up late in the morning, and when I do wake up I lie in bed for quite a while before I get out of bed. When I do get out of bed, I eat a leisurely breakfast. I enjoy my breakfast, and I look out the window at the birds and the woods. I feel better these days. I have more time to write songs.

I go into my room and I take out my guitar. I strap my guitar onto myself and I strum chords until I feel the special vibrations. Sometimes I have a glass of water when I play my guitar. I strum the chords and I sing the words that pop into my mind. I sing things like *oh my, I want some food, food can make me feel so good, because I know that eating makes me, eating makes me, fascinates me, every time I eat the food I like I think of other food, and pancakes are the food I like, but I like other food as well* and I record it all on a series of machines in my office. I work all day on my songs.

When I break for lunch, I bring the microphone with me and I record my eating. I've built up a vast archive of the sounds of my eating. Mostly I eat sandwiches, so it sounds like a lot of soft chewing. If I use crisp lettuce on my sandwich, that changes the sound. It sounds more bright and snappy with the lettuce. BLTs have a very exciting sound, especially when the bacon is well done. When the bread is toasted, that obviously changes the entire frequency range of the recording. For a while I was interested in reverb and echo, and I added a lot of different echoes to the recordings of lunch. During this period my lunches began to sound like old Phil Spector recordings. It's like the Wall of Sound of Lunch. If Phil Spector had kept the tape rolling while the Ronettes broke for lunch, I imagine that it would sound like this. But soon enough, I started thinking about the commercial music business and all the effects and compression and reverb and everything, and I went back to recording my lunch dry. It's not the effects that make the lunch. It's the act of eating lunch that is important. Putting a microphone next to lunch is all it takes. I will not alter the sound of lunch with studio trickery just to satisfy some record executive with a Rolls Royce and gold teeth. If the sound is different, it's because the food is different. I eat chips, and chips sound different from Twizzlers. Twizzlers sound different from fresh fruit. Drinking a glass of water is an entirely different kind of sound. When I finish my lunch, I go back to my office and record my songs.

The thing that worries me is that all my lyrics lately are about food. Nothing else pops into my mind. So I'm thinking of maybe doing a concept album with eating noises and songs about food. I don't think that would be too commercial, so it's all right. But it needs to make a little money, because I just quit my job. But it can't be too commercial. I'm thinking of calling it, "The Sounds of Lunch."

## Stop Writing to Jazz

Related self matrix modulation
The rapid pen sat capturing the tongue
Rinsing in mid-drought
The cannibal way you crave me

Why can't you walk slowly?
Why won't you sit down
And breathe with me?
Lay yourself down on the earth
No saxophone music
Stop writing to jazz

You car horn reptilicus
Fighting the flu
I badly wax sad
I'm a fraud and a red

Chinchillas run scared
And birds in the city
Get sucked into fans
We relate to
And hate to
Admit to
Ideas about living
Crawling in dirt

Statues of animals scattered in fields

In cities on roads

Reminding us here of our will to forget.

# Sing Sweetly

Bereft and becleft
Besmirched and besmeared
My eyelets and baubles now burst from their bags
Move wicked and backwards
And thrust into me

My cowardice twitching
All balled up and retching
I made myself useful
I sat in the back
And you sipping tea
With your big-boned persona

Sing sweetly and tell me
You don't want to hear
My butt-load of worries
My hogshead of fears

# And rubber skin Buddha sits plainly on eggshells

Disguising the fact that his payments are late
And the laundry is piling up higher than Crosby
Drunker than priests on a day full of masses

Kept like a virgin and cut like a razor
Bloodied-up sheets and a head full of bourbon
Lighter then darker then absolute nowhere
Stuck on a hook in a bucket of bait

Children in heavy coats crouched under windows
Big twitching mandibles splashing in bathtubs
Savory chicken breasts stuffed with no sympathy
It's time we get packing and head for Tibet

Croutons and apricots tossed with the laundry
Women with duffle bags walking home wet
The stomachs of salesmen digesting their paychecks
It's time we get packing and head for Tibet

# Sunday Service

From time to time I agree to give a concert at my mother's church. My mother is an Episcopalian, and although live performance is not my forte, I do believe in lending my talents now and then for the greater good of the community. Also, the church pays me fifty dollars to do a short concert, followed by a fifteen-minute Q&A.

This week my mother asks if I'll consider sitting in with the organist and choir for a Sunday service. The choir director, a man named Steven Took, is an adventurous sort, always looking for new ways to expand and energize the liturgical soundscape. He decided that a bit of percussion would help liven things up and wanted to know if I would bring a bunch of my instruments and gadgets to accompany the group. My mother assures me that I will have complete creative control over all percussion arrangements, and if it works out, we can explore the possibility of incorporating my work regularly into the church's repertoire.

I am not a man of God. The idea of organized religion has always struck me as absurd, misguided, and even pathological, but my mother finds great comfort in church activities—her knitting group, her Bible study, her Tuesday pot-lucks—so I try to keep my views to myself. On the rare occasions that I do go to church with my mother, I refuse to chant along with any creeds or prayers. To my ear, the parishioners' monotone drone sounds more like the dark hymnal of Satan than holy worship. I get the shivers when they say things like, "We look for the resurrection of the dead," or, "We bewail our manifold sins and wickedness."

I am willing, though, to sing along with church songs because, for me, music is the least offensive part of any church service. After all, much of the music in the Episcopal tradition comes from great composers like Beethoven, Mendelssohn, or Bach, and the lyrics from such poets as Milton, Herbert, and Donne. That's why, when my mother asks, I agree to perform at the next Sunday service. One could do worse than to shake maracas and bang cymbals to the works of the greatest creative minds in Western culture. Also, my mother says the church will pay seventy-five dollars for my time and effort.

Using my mother as courier, Steven Took sends me a draft program for the service and a set of sheet music covering all the hymns and prayer songs. I do not read music, so the sheets are useless to me. Luckily, though, my mother has an uncanny memory for hymns and prayer songs. It takes a little needling, but I finally convince her to sing each melody into a microphone in my home recording studio. The poor woman is extremely self-conscious about her voice, and she makes me agree *in writing* not to play back any of the recordings while she is still within earshot.

Listening to the melodies over and over in my headphones, I familiarize myself with their contours and textures. Eventually, I am able to create a bold but tasteful percussion arrangement for each. Some songs seem to require a strong backbeat, while others only call for occasional ornaments, flourishes, and accents to intensify their dynamic range. I even work out a few synthesizer parts— rhythmical bleeps and blips to give a couple of the tunes a more contemporary flare. Grafting my own musical ideas onto these antiquated compositions, I feel as if I have tapped into the rhythms of a distant past, and that I am leaving my own mark on a sacred tradition of music that has spanned centuries and which will endure for centuries to come. Never have I gotten so close to a set of songs, dived so deeply into their melodies and cadences, understood so implicitly their bold lines and subtle shadings. Sitting in my office with headphones on and a cowbell in hand, I sense for the first time in my life the presence of a benevolent spirit, a higher power. I wonder to myself, is God here in these songs? When Saturday evening arrives I put the finishing touches on my arrangements, pack my instruments and gadgets into a crate, and lay out my best Sunday suit.

Steven Took fidgets with his conductor's baton and smiles brightly as I set up my instruments on a small table in the organ loft. He has grown a beard since the last time I saw him. The choir, made up mostly of women in their middle age, assembles in a semi-circle around me. They are astonished that I have memorized all of the songs, and that I will play my part without the aid of sheet music. After some final preparations and a few words of advice from Steven, we all join hands and bow our heads in prayer. Normally a group prayer like this would make me squirm, but this morning I am simply glad for the assurance that God will guide my performance, and that if only I will entrust myself to His loving embrace, all will be as it should be.

Amen.

The church hushes as parishioners make their way to the pews. The organ prelude is a piece by Salzburg, the textures of which I am able to deepen with a subtle combination of maracas and train whistle. Immediately, the place buzzes with excitement. People turn to see the source of these unconventional sounds, whisper to each other, giggle joyfully.

I reserve my musical grand entrance for the opening hymn, "Holy Spirit, Font of Light," and when it begins I can feel shockwaves rippling through the chapel. With each rim shot, bass beat, and synthesized chirp, I feel the miracle of creation in my heavenly soul. This is God's music, I think, and as the song progresses through its first and second verses I give myself up to the vibrations of divine inspiration. The congregation swoons. They turn and stare with their mouths agape. As the service charges ahead, I improvise wildly through the offertory anthem, through "Glory to God in the Highest," and through the post-communion hymn. With each tune, I feel more strongly the presence of the Holy Ghost in my instruments. When we arrive at the final hymn, I am aflame with the Spirit of the Lord. The sounds that burst from my humble corner of the organ loft transcend all earthly limits. I channel the cosmos. I breach the divide between body and spirit. No one is more surprised than I am by the spontaneous blasts and sonic eruptions emitting from my instruments, my gadgets, and my own throat. I step outside of myself. I howl. I groan. I am ecstatic. I am awash in God's battering riptide!

When it is finished, the entire place seems to exhale in unison. No one says a word. Apparently the priest has decided to forego the dismissal. The parishioners, clergy, and choir members file out of the chapel. Finally, I am alone with Steven Took, who strokes his beard and looks at the floor. "That was quite something," he says. "Really something." I pack my things and leave.

It's been almost a week since the service, and I haven't heard from Steven Took. But what is there to say, really? My mother assures me that the performance was well received by all, but I have my doubts. In fact, I've become suspicious of the entire affair. Was that God's grace I felt coursing through my veins? Or was I simply caught up in a grand deception, mistaking my own natural enthusiasm for divine intervention? Maybe it doesn't matter.

When my mother hands me a thank-you card from the choir, I am glad to find seventy-five dollars in cash tucked neatly inside.

"Thank God," I say, and my mother swells with pride.

# Sipping on Spring

Sipping on spring
I sink my teeth
into a fleshy egg

Cuticle hairdo
killing me softly
with his tongs

Back door ballet
sniffing up incense
snuff and cocaine

Relaxing backwards
stiff in a new shirt
propped up and shaking

Throwing her leg
up over my shoulder
pop out a muscle

Lying out flat
pills and whiskey
heating pad rash

Summer invades
I pull down the shade
sink back and wait

# I Am Here To Make Fun of Poetry

The way Walt Whitman changed the line and
Sylvia's cold blast of an oven-mitt firecracker dark shoehorn
bastard sandwich with my own shapely tie, furrowed and
wilted like a "much madness is divinest sense"-icle pop-cone
bandage for Li Po's appointment book budget.


Stanzas and line breaks and stanzas and line breaks and stanzas and
    line breaks and


if you want an impenetrable backstop of a fueled canticle lemon,
    then
you've come to the wrong placemat grease stain. And besides, the
    performance
has been over for centuries.


Hitler!


I am choking on a dinner-plate backbone, in-
voking a Kama Sutra title page, re-
stoking a mouth-ulcer fire cake, and ra-
king myself under damp dirt obscurity for the benefit of Mr.
Wallace Ste-
vens.

Even me, leaving steep features, pleading with creatures to beach me

    like a white

whale on Ishmael's hidden tale,

beset with hypos,

braving November's stale Plato,

and needling Socrates to swallow the hemlock milkshake,

for God's sake.

# The Tower

Take a seat. Do you want a drink? Here, use a coaster. Mmm, that's it. Loosen your tie. Put on these glasses. Do you see all the individual objects now? Sit closer to me. Do you need a pen? Write your name down. Nice.

What's that? Do you hear that? Look, the table's shaking. The windows are rattling. Do you feel it? Poor thing, you look scared. Don't worry. I've been here for a long time and nothing bad ever happens. Close your eyes. Imagine you're floating somewhere. Think about shapes and colors. Come on now, I want to see a smile. Yeah, that's it. Doesn't it feel better when you smile?

I have some photos to show you. They're right here in this album. You know I have them all organized. Do you remember this? There you are. It's kind of hard to see, but if you look closely— see? Right there. In the sky. Do you remember that? You went pretty high up that day. No rope. No safety net. Just suspended there. That was a great day.

Are you cold? Here, put on this hat. Want some cocoa? Let's light a fire. How's that? Too much? Is it all too much? Just sit back. Here are some mittens. I knitted these. Put them on. Nice. Hold your legs up. Let me get you into this snowsuit. There you go. Now lean forward. Give me your arms. Do want me to zip the hood? How's that? You look happy.

What's that? Were you going to say something? Are you sure? You can say something. No? You're being shy. You were always shy. So quiet. Quiet and shy. Out in the backyard, keeping yourself busy. I hardly knew you were there.

You want a cracker? Go ahead, I have a lot of crackers. That's right. Here's a napkin. You're getting crumbs all over. That's alright. I need to clean this place anyway. You want some broth? I made it from scratch. Take a sip. You've never had broth like this. It's the best broth. The best god damn broth. Man, it's good.

Hey, look at that. You see the tower? I look up at that tower every morning. I wake up and it's the first thing I see. What do you think that tower's for? Electricity? Radio? What kind of signals are coming out of that tower? Do you know? Hey, don't get mad. Here. Put on these slippers. I won't talk about the tower anymore. Let's talk about you. Look at you. You're so sweet and kind. Look at your eyeballs. So smooth. Oh man. Does your head hurt? My head hurts. How about your throat? Wow, my knuckles are sore. Every day it gets worse. Do you have it, too? Maybe it's that tower. Oh, I don't know. So many invisible things. Do you ever feel that? Invisible things. Like rays. Sound waves. Particles. Zoom! Sssstttvvvv! Zhssa!

I'm sorry. Are you upset now? Lie back. Close your eyes. Look at your skin. It's all over the couch. That's okay. Here, bite down on this. Do you feel dizzy?

# From Fetal to Fecal: A Memoir

*I. The Pet Peeves of the Dead*

A red hat made in Paris by a sailor who didn't know any better, and he claims to have come from Brooklyn. Brooklyn. Cat o'nine tails and a quick walk through neighborhoods from your past and fat boy friends who never get sleep and they wink and blink in the bright day walk past sign post dinner time underwear head back eat late put grease feet now bit rate scum lick blink in the middle with hot cat steam and a brandy-wine tree.

"didn't you know that?" bugged out face and a mist breath and a self-bloat caravan niceties put forth and retracted according to applause meters and potential for hot soup and a nice meal.

"no. as a matter of fact I didn't. look, you've got something in your teeth. it's disgusting." I hate it. I hate what's in your teeth, and also I hate your teeth. Your very teeth, which click and grind in a way that repulses me, gnaws at the pit of my stomach. "and those pants you're wearing. stolen from pygmies!"

At this you storm away, leaving me by myself which is never can't seed bag waiting for a true suitcase that never comes, and me restless and assimilating. And me on fire like this. And me.

*II. Starting on Solids*

stained pink
and round
like steak

stabbed, my liquified organs
shrink back,
evaporate from the sand
and blacktop.

Turncoat scrotal skin flake membrane,
like a stick insect
like a silly shirt
like puking green
in silhouette
on the telephone.

heavy levitation
very contagious
five-point pen
    erasing procedures
mix music with zen
capable caveman
relates to the greats
he camps on a cone
    on a cliff with a scone

smoking in the back

he's a solid citizen

*III. A Useless Mantra*

"He kept buying raspberry squares and taking notes on them and putting them in plastic bags and flattening them under the big dictionary and storing them in an airtight room in the basement of an old theatre."

*IV. Death by Kitty Litter*

Crap catching spatula

Bastards on ice

Finicky lickers

Faster and quicker

Bedtime for everyone

Down with your dirt

Fancily rancid

Broken and hurt

*V. How the Hunger Smelled*

Stomach empty and head removed. Spine slithering alone in the back of the room, dehydrated and weary from walking. This natural disaster. This comprehensive mishap compliments of a complete misunderstanding.

Which membrane do I activate? Which membrane? Which am I? Why have I faded from this picture? My inner toad hops rhythmically, but to what end? Am I moot? This difficulty is manifest in yeast rising and peculiar smells lingering and then fading like smoke from a significant settlement. My anger and sadness mix to produce an alienating odor.

wilted. barely fascinated by the glittery gleam of yellow light on wet black ink.

# I Require

I require savory stuffing,
hot brittle sandwiches,
succulent strudel,
and broiled baby animal.

I require wet-scented napkins
and cold-frosted silverware.

I require deep-fried hard candy,
squashed ham with loaf,
and one breathing head held against another,
warm like a baby's head,
nose whistling inhale.

# The Tragedy in My Neighborhood

I didn't sleep last night. I stayed up typing. It's simple to get to sunrise. Last night I typed all night. I kept typing and now I've got fifty-two pages folded up in a box.

My virtuous acts today are worth mentioning. I held the door for a woman at the front entrance to the building. Inside the building, I threw some scrap paper into the recycling bin. I met the new man and congratulated him. I stepped outdoors to have a smoke. I appreciated the sky and the tips of tree branches. I breathed the air and showed my teeth to people in their cars.

The stack of books on my desk is growing. I check books out of the library. The stack of books has been growing. The books are mostly collections of critical essays on the nineteenth-century author Hilda Lydia Sanchez. Hilda Lydia Sanchez lived in the southwestern United States in the late-nineteenth century. Very few people know the works of Hilda Lydia Sanchez. It's an interest of mine. Like the tragedy that happened in my neighborhood. It's an interest of mine.

The tragedy that happened in my neighborhood was in all the papers and on television. A neighbor of mine lost hope. He said he lost hope in front of the mirror. I found him outside his house. He sat in a lawn chair. I said, "You're okay?" He said, "No." He sat outside his burning house. I asked where the others were. He didn't say anything. I tried my hardest to enter the house, but it was impossible. I remember thinking that I should type about this.

I typed my thoughts today. It's the first time I ever tried. It was harder than I thought. Every time I thought I was really typing my thoughts it turned out I wasn't. I pulled hair out of my head. I kept typing until it was my thoughts. What I typed was interesting, but only to me. At the end of the day I folded up the typed sheets of paper and put them in a box. I thought about stepping outside to smoke and breathe the air, but then I decided to smoke inside. While I smoked I looked out the window. The house next door was black and charred. Half of it had collapsed. I turned out the light and looked hard. I thought I saw the neighbor's lawn chair, but it was too dark and so I couldn't be sure.

Hilda Lydia Sanchez wrote three novels, but not one of them was published during her lifetime. She died young. Her mother always told her not to write. She told Hilda Lydia to spend more time mending the neighbors' clothes, but Hilda Lydia would not stop writing. She wrote about people she wished she could be. Hilda Lydia's mother said she spent too much time dreaming. After Hilda Lydia died, her mother read what her daughter had written. She cried and she felt like she finally understood. But it was too late.

At work I helped the new man to understand his job. He was having some trouble. I lied and told him that when I started I didn't understand anything about the job, either. He said that made him feel better, and I showed him the forms and the slots and the correct way to print the reports. I saw his lips move, silently repeating the things I said. After lunch the new man felt better. He practiced and said he felt more comfortable. I told him he made it look easy. I told him he was doing a good job. But then the new man made a mistake that revealed his stupidity. I told him it was okay, but I knew it really wasn't.

I tried typing at home, but the men and the trucks were too loud. I sat for a while listening to the men and the trucks. They were cleaning up the tragedy. I put on my coat and stepped outside, pretending that it was to smoke. But really I wanted to watch the men and the trucks. One of the men looked at me while I lit up my smoke. I tried to wave but I knocked my smoke into the snow and I almost fell over. The man looked away and continued to clean up. They used one machine to knock it all down and another machine to pick it all up and then the trucks to take it all away.

My face was shaking today. I ran to the restroom. My face turned red and my mouth showed teeth. I saw myself in the mirror next to the clock and ran to the restroom before the new man saw me. On the way to the restroom I stopped and held the door for a woman from the first floor. I stopped and held the door. The woman smiled at me and didn't notice anything about the shaking. In the restroom I made sure I was alone. I held my face and spoke to myself until the shaking stopped. When the shaking stopped I returned to my desk. The new man asked me to check over his work, and it was all wrong. I told him it was okay.

After the death of Hilda Lydia Sanchez, her mother vowed to publish her work. She spent all her spare time writing letters and sending manuscripts. Hilda Lydia's mother learned all about the publishing industry. She traveled across the country to New York City and visited publishers in their offices. She made up stories about her dead daughter. She said whatever she thought she needed to say. She said it to their beards. She begged. She yelled. She cried. After two years she found a publisher for her daughter's first novel, *The Man Who Sold Houses*. A year later it was bound and released to the public The novel earned a modicum of critical praise. It didn't sell. Hilda Lydia's mother spent the next three years trying to sell her daughter's second novel, *The Affluent Family*.

I typed the story of Hilda Lydia Sanchez. I typed about what the critics said. I tried to type my thoughts but it was hard. Outside, the men smoothed the ground where the tragedy had happened. I typed about the men and how they cleaned up. I typed the story of the mother of Hilda Lydia. New men with ties and hats brought new machines. I couldn't type my thoughts so I went outside for a smoke. I waved carefully at the new men and they waved back. I asked them what they planned to do, but the machines were too loud. I stepped inside the house. My phone was ringing. It was the new man.

What I did for the new man is worth mentioning. I told the boss that his work was improving. I said I thought the new man should have another chance. I agreed to work closely with the new man until his output improved. The boss said she was counting on me. She said the new man had caused plenty of grief. It was up to me to make things right again. I looked for the new man at his desk, but he wasn't there. I found him in the lunch room writing a letter. He said he was very angry, and he had decided to quit. I told him that the boss wanted him off the premises immediately. The new man became enraged.

In my neighborhood the children sometimes play in the road.

Today I watched them play a game in the half-built house on the lot where the tragedy happened. They ran up and down the new stairs. They leapt through the spaces where the walls were not yet built. A bigger child knocked down a smaller child. The bigger child held the smaller child down under a piece of scrap lumber. Some of the children ran off when the smaller child began to cry. Four children stayed and threw pebbles at the smaller child and laughed. The smaller child shrieked and squirmed. He couldn't free himself. Next, the bigger child gathered a handful of sand and rubbed it into the smaller child's face. I smoked inside and typed on sheets of paper until my thoughts scattered. I folded them up and put them in a box.

Hilda Lydia Sanchez wrote every morning after chores. She used a quill pen that she made herself. She also made her own paper. She bought ink with the little money she earned from mending the neighbors' clothes. Hilda Lydia's mother told her not to write. Once she burned several sheets of Hilda Lydia's paper in the fireplace. But Hilda Lydia never raised her voice to her mother, and she always completed her chores. She kept her written pages locked in a box after that. No matter how hard she tried, Hilda Lydia's mother could never find the key. She had to break the lock after Hilda Lydia died. When she read her daughter's writing she felt like it was her own thoughts on paper. She knew she couldn't burn it. How could she burn her own thoughts?

The new man only hurt three people at work. The boss, the secretary, and the receptionist. He sat in the lobby and cried until the police came. The police handled him roughly. The new man said he had only one friend in the building. He pointed at me. When the police dragged him away, he spit and swore and kicked at the doorjamb. It was quiet afterwards, and I tried to stop my face from shaking. I walked quickly to the restroom. Nobody noticed. In the restroom I looked at my face, red with teeth showing. I thought of Hilda Lydia Sanchez and wished I could type my thoughts. I wanted to type in the restroom. I held my head with both hands and closed my eyes. Someone entered the bathroom. I heard footsteps. I heard, "You're okay?" I opened my eyes and couldn't stop the shaking. I showed teeth. I said, "This is what it's like."

# Eating

I cleanse my palette,
uvula and glottis delightfully refreshed,
tongue rippling muscular and wet, segmented.

Cornucopia of razor blades,
each cactus swallow scream,
lip split to chin, secret teeth revealed!

I chew my palette,
grind it into paste and swish.
This drink of deception,
this sensory milkshake.

At table I spit into paper cup.
While napping, I rewind the day.

Such tainted visions!
What fiendish cud!

# The Theatre of Cruelty

We were on holiday when Abbey ate
the Word. She sort of lifted it and put
it in her mouth, she hadn't cleaned her plate;
she'd only just arrived, stomped her foot
one time, chewed and swallowed hard. I held
my breath and watched her struggle with the thing.

It wasn't long before the dinner bell
rang out. We all began to shout and sing
our joyful songs. When Abbey's face turned blue
we softened to a hum. She grabbed her throat
and pulled a chair down as she fell. We knew
enough to stop our singing when she spoke.

"I thought a Word could nourish me," she said.
Before she spoke another she was dead.

# Expecting

This morning the broad strokes of heaven
stick like electrodes to my paper skin;
two cats glide over my desk,
one tears at the living room carpet.

Outside, the traffic scatters a cloud of egg steam,
and motors seize and burn, ooze their insides out.

All door handles rattle loose
in my cracked hands. The shock
of another day glues itself to the pavement.

You sleep in an anthill
of pillows and kind prayers
while twin butterflies circle the telephone pole
outside our window.

What was it you said last night?

Ear pressed to your swollen belly, I heard
the tiny knuckles of language
kneading a slippery syntax,
paradiddling our racing thoughts,

knocking to get out.

# A Day in the Life of a Conversationalist

He awoke precisely at sunrise and slowly, deliberately inflated his head. He reached for the controls and, finding them, manipulated his way out of bed and headed for the washroom. In the washroom he set about scrubbing and shaving his slender neck. His head naturally expanded and contracted during this process. While shaving he thought of his gardens and the joy they brought him. He remembered wonderful meals and pondered thought-scanners. His dear friend operated a thought-scanning machine for the government; he wondered if it had ever been used as part of a practical joke. He finished shaving his neck and then leaned over to drain the excess jelly from his sinus.

Smiling, he felt glad to be embarking on another night of work as a conversationalist. He enjoyed his job. He thought talking was the most stimulating of activities. He always kept his neck cleanly shaven, and he always listened intently when engaged in conversation. He had a knack for setting his conversation partners at ease. He leaned lovingly toward them, his lavender ears twitching with intention. As a professional conversationalist, he had to know the secret ways around and into the minds of his clients.

"Are you warm now?"

"No. Are you?"

"I'm slightly warm. But if you're comfortable, let's talk about your family's wagon."

"Oh yes, the wagon. It's been in our family for years. Every autumn we lubricate the poles and scour the gliding apparatus."

"Is it a lark each time?"

"Yes, it's a lark. And that's what I love about my family. Something so dull as a seasonal wagon lubrication and scouring can become an occasion for sincere mirth and copulating. It's always a lark."

"Are you warm now?"

"Yes, now I am a bit warm."

"I'll go and regulate the temperature."

"Thank you. I'll take some more drink and a raisin square, if you don't mind."

He was always generous with his raisin squares, and he always maintained an ideal temperature at the office.

On the way home from work, he tried to remember the last time he had his wagon lubricated and scoured. It had been a while. He would visit the scouring station soon.

He switched on the radio.


In the afternoon he visited his young nephew in prison. He paused at the prison door and plucked a rose from the massive bush that grew there. The prison was a very unpleasant place, and his young nephew had done some very unpleasant things.

Upon entering the building, he was accosted by three or four metal arms, each employing a thoroughly intrusive device that ensured prison guests were not concealing weapons or food or scraps of paper for passing secret messages. When he had been prodded and frisked by the metal arms, he moved forward to the thought-scanning machine. This always scared him, because he had heard that if he were ever found to have even the hint of an escape plot in his head, he would be shocked violently through his lavender ears and detained in a body booth for a minimum of four to six weeks. Of course, he would never think of trying to break his young nephew out of such an impenetrable and smothering place— the very idea was ludicrous. Nonetheless he became frightfully nervous each time he entered the thought-scanning area. What if the machine were to misread his thoughts? He hated to think of the awful shock that would be applied to his tender ears, not to mention the inconvenience of being detained for such a long time without any conversation. For in prison, no inmate can speak or even move.

Each inmate is confined to a body booth. The booth fits snugly around the contours of the inmate's body. It is made of a soft, rubbery material that both extracts and replaces moisture for the body. The genitals rest in a small pocket of netting, and the prisoners' fingers and toes are allowed to protrude from the booth so that they are relatively unrestricted, although each digit is attached, by a sort of leathery string, to a series of levers and pulleys controlled by the prison's central controlling machine. When an inmate, whose thoughts were continually monitored through the body booth's head piece, was found to be actively pursuing objectionable ideas in his mind, the prison's controlling machine was capable of administering a strangely electric, yet entirely mysterious brand of discipline through these dangling, leathery strings.

He cleared the thought-scanning booth with no incident, and

he moved into the waiting area. Here, he was assigned a chair, as he was each morning, and he sat down and waited for his number to be called. After a minute or so, his number was called out over the loudspeaker, and he proceeded to the long hall. He knew exactly how far to walk before he would arrive at the viewing area of his young nephew. For five minutes (ten minutes on state holidays) he was allowed to gaze at the face of his young nephew, which protruded awkwardly from the rubbery material of his body booth. His young nephew, like all the prisoners, had a bilious complexion due to the unnatural process of bodily fluid extraction and replacement effected by the confining booth. He gazed pitifully at his young nephew, who always managed to make eye contact and sometimes even to eke out what might be loosely termed a facial expression, for which he was invariably punished by the strangely pulsating leathery strings dangling from his fingers and toes. Most facial expressions were almost always the result of some disallowed thought process, and punishment was instantaneous.

When his five minutes (ten minutes on state holidays) were up, he broke eye contact with his young nephew and made his way to the exit.

To relax, he caressed his long, lavender ears. His webbing sagged and he sighed. He was exhausted. He felt sorry for his young nephew. He felt sorry for himself. Briefly, he practiced solo-conversation. "This world," he said aloud. But then he thought, no. He paused. "O this weary world." That's not it, he thought to himself. He shut his eyes for a moment to let the jelly ooze out of his sinus.

He felt sleep creeping up. Quickly he worked the controls. With his eyes shut tight he said, "I am not full of fear this evening." Then somewhat awkwardly, "I'm not." And then, after a second of silence, "I'm not." And his head collapsed, filling his nocturnal breathing apparatus with sparkling vapor, and he drifted gently to sleep.

He dreamt, as always, of music. And in his dream, as always, he had a brother with whom he co-owned a giant gymnasium. He and his brother, lacking any exercise or recreational equipment, simply ran up and down the length of the gymnasium. The room was vast, and their loud footsteps made a hollow echo.

He awoke suddenly and his soft head inflated. He checked the time. Six hours had passed. He became anxious for a moment, but his tension soon gave way to glad reveries. He imagined himself upside down, suspended from a tree limb. He imagined himself falling from a great height. He stretched his legs in bed. He envisioned a great, flaming sky wheel. His webbing contracted and then sagged.

He slept.

# Quote/Unquote

"The man who approached me in the theatre lobby and asked, 'Did you hear about the woman who was in here earlier saying, "My psychologist was exactly correct when she advised, 'Don't listen to people who say, "You've got to follow these instructions, which read, 'Always listen when your mother says, "You've got that look on your face that means you're thinking, 'Why do I have to put up with my parents when they shout, "Don't you dare stand there with that look on your face mumbling, 'I hate you,' because we can hear every word!" I mean, it's so unfair,' and you can just forget it right now," because she knows what she's talking about,' or else you'll screw it all up," because they don't understand who you are,' and of course that's what I pay her for," before she demanded a refund and stormed out?' and then didn't even wait for me to answer before he left the theatre himself and walked off, staring at the sky."

# Life Lessons

Father died in a fire when I was five, brother
tried to choke himself on the ashes, upturning
the decorative urn, soiling the carpet,
blackening his face and neck.

Mother supported us by winning radio contests, bursting
through busy phone lines, extracting answers from her magic purse:
"Saber-toothed tiger!" "The electric light bulb!"
"Five thousand, five hundred and five dollars, and fifty-five cents!"

Five of my fingers became sensitive, squirming tendrils.
On graduation day I cried and became shy, failed
to live up to the promise I'd shown
as a boy.

Kitty slapped me five once, after hours
of instruction, and this was my greatest pedagogical triumph.
But she never did it again, no matter how hard
I begged. She just grinned at me, grinned at me,
always grinning after that. Always.

# Cat Soup

## I.

I sit in the dark corner with my sister cooking cat soup—the cruelest soup—and my sister begs me for two dollars and a tank of gas and the keys to my car. "No," I say. And then, "Go away!" But soon I relent and hand over the keys, and I find myself also handing her my lunchbox—precious, doted-on lunchbox, lunchbox of my wildest dreams—and she grabs it out of my hand and leaves me weeping into my barebones ham-and-plastic-bag sandwich.

I feel so alone, stirring soup in the dark corner.

My sister returns and tells me to butter the bread and put on some music. I obey, but only because she threatens me with her menacing looks. "It's time for soup," she whispers. And then she shouts, "MOTHER!"

Oh, our dear mother. Our dear mother who tries so hard. She springs from the basement and joins us in the dark corner for cat soup. She compliments my sister and me. She encourages us and coos and purrs. With a quick sweep of her hand she irons the wrinkles from her blue-and-yellow pattern dress. She stands erect like a hat-tree, and for a brief moment we are a family. We eat the soup until it's gone, and then we clean our faces with carefully unfolded cloth napkins. Our mother recedes into the basement.

My sister fixes her gaze on me. "Hand over that sandwich, Simon."

I hesitate. I withdraw the bag-and-ham sandwich from my jacket pocket and make a desperate attempt to swallow it whole.

My sister lunges at me and punches my Adam's apple. I cough up the plastic bag and its half-chewed contents. I can't catch my breath. The smell of ham.

## 2.

I find keys in the ignition of my car and suddenly I am driving. I loosen my necktie. My lunchbox is here. It is a bright summer day. I make my way to the municipal park where I imagine a solitary picnic might help clear my head. I shudder at the thought of my sister's cat soup. I switch on the radio.

At the park entrance I am forced to pay two dollars to a lithe young lady in a brown, clapboarded booth. I know well enough that my car is an eyesore, and so her incredulous stare is moot. I point to my lunchbox and declare my intention to picnic. She hands me my change and a park map and waves me in. I leave a mess of paint chips and rust in my wake as I gratefully plunge into the park's manufactured effulgence.

Steering happily toward my favorite picnic area I am shocked to find that my familiar spot has been razed and replaced with a wretched, utterly ridiculous baseball complex. I ease off the accelerator and gaze, open-mouthed at this obscene development. Spoiled, dim-witted children in short pants scamper back and forth, throw balls at each other, and chew blankly on their leather mitts. Overexcited adults shriek from shiny metal bleachers, hike up their khaki pants, and swill dark soda from plastic cups. How many years has it been since I visited the municipal park?

Coasting along, I fly into a panic and shout, "Ridiculous!" My mood worsens. A large sign hanging from an endless stretch of chain link fence reads: SPORTSPLEX. This is the spot where I used to picnic. I pull my car to the curb and switch off the radio. "Hapless!" I shout, but no one hears me. My picnic table! My shady glen! A lone, metal bench stands directly beneath the menacing sign. Determined to picnic in my favorite spot, I head for the bench.

In my lunchbox is a mess of plastic bags and chunks of hot ham. My thermos is too tightly capped. I struggle to open it, but the constant clanking of bats on balls sends shivers through me and saps my strength. I give up. I slump and sag. My lunchbox falls and its contents empty onto the grass.

Suddenly, an endearing little black kitten appears and begins nosing through my ham and plastic bags. He is skin and bones and his backside is rough with mange. I give him a searching look and our eyes meet; he blurts a scratchy meow. I am touched. "Will you share a picnic with me?" The kitten bites ravenously at greasy plastic. He smells ham. I am overcome. "Endearing kitten, you are a breath of fresh air." Tears stream down my cheeks. I make a new attempt to pry the lid off of my thermos. It takes every bit of strength I have to wrestle the cap loose. When it finally budges, the thermos seems to collapse in my hand, exhaling all of its steaming contents into the open air. What is this? My sister has played the cruelest joke of all. She has filled my thermos with cat soup.

The kitten yelps and springs backwards, scalded by the broth. "Oh no!" I shout, leaping to my feet and dropping the thermos. The kitten recedes, frightened and confused. "No, no." I grab up a plastic bag and follow the poor feline as it scampers toward the batting cage. "I didn't mean any harm." It retreats at top speed from me now. The batting cage's chain-link door is wide open, and the kitten runs straight in. My heart sinks. Monstrous, gear-grinding mechanical pitching arms hurl hard balls toward helmeted youths wielding aluminum bats. The kitten darts back and forth in a panic. I enter the batting cage and attempt to save the poor thing. I hold out the greasy bag. "Kitty! The ham! The ham!" The kitten freezes for a moment, glances at me, and then dashes for the back of the cage and disappears behind the dreadful pitching machines.

I am nearly pelted by countless fastballs. Crouching, clutching my bag of ham, blind with fear, I practically crawl to the back of the cage. I see the kitten now, edging dangerously close to the foreboding gears of the pitching machine. I reach out my shaking arm. I whisper excitedly, "Ham!" And then, "Kitty!"

For a moment, it looks as if the kitten might leap willingly into the chaos of sharp metal teeth and tormenting gears. "Please," I implore, opening the plastic bag now and offering a small bit of ham. It works. The kitten steps gingerly away from the machine and noses up to my outstretched hand. Just as it snatches the ham from my fingers, I grab hold of the kitten with my free hand.

I stand up straight and search for a safe way out of the batting cage. But the kitten, struck with absolute fear for its life, sinks its fangs into the flesh between my thumb and index finger. I try to let go, but the kitten plunges its teeth again and again into my bleeding hand. I run straight for the door, the kitten now firmly attached to my arm. The spray of fastballs is relentless, and before I can manage my escape I am struck in the head. I hear the shrieking voices of entitled youths. The world goes dark. The smell of ham.

### 3.

My head swims. My hand is wrapped in gauze. I am questioned by the police. It is blindingly bright.

"Now what did you say the cat looked like?"

"Kitten. It was a kitten."

"Now why did you pick up the cat?"

"It was in danger."

He laughs. I hear a woman laughing in the background.

"Where am I?" I look around and realize that this is the hospital.

"Gee, I'm sorry. Now why don't you relax? It'll be awhile before the nurse is ready to give you your shot." He winks at the woman and smiles.

"Where is my lunchbox? How did I get here?"

"Now I've got to fill out a report before we let you go on your way. Your sister will be down to pick you up as soon as we're through."

"My sister?"

"Now we didn't manage to catch the kitty cat that attacked you. It receded into that municipal drain. We think it lives in there."

"The soup!" I cry. "The soup! Where is my lunchbox? It is imperative that I find my lunchbox!"

When I stand up, the officer restrains me. He makes a signal, and quickly I am pinned down by a number of flexing arms. I gaze at the stark white ceiling and despair that my picnic was so hideously thwarted. A nurse appears and she sinks a shiny needle into my arm. I feel sick, then light as a feather, and before long I recede into a dark corner. The smell of ham.

### 4.

"MOTHER!" My sister stirs the soup. She smiles and helps me up from my bed. "He's awake now, Mother!"

At the dinner table, our mother makes positive remarks. She encourages us and recounts our youthful successes. I feel nauseous. My arm is numb and cold. My sister ladles cat soup into deep, dark bowls. She hands me a spoon.

"Please, no soup," I say. "Can't I have ham?" My stomach stirs and lurches.

"Animal Control recommends that you eat nothing but soup until your series of shots is complete."

I shrug.

"I suppose you know it was wrong for you to go to the park."

I pat my pockets. The keys to my car are gone. My lunchbox is lost. I feign a look of gratitude, which seems to please our mother; she claps her hands together lightly. I fix my gaze on three or four plastic bags of ham on the table beside my sister's bowl. Reluctantly I dip my spoon into the soup—the cruelest soup—and we eat until it's gone.

# This Poem

This poem is about my father, who raised me on a small farm in northwestern Connecticut and whose sternness and magnanimous disinterest have always been an inspiration as well as a serious obstacle to my development as a human being.

This poem is written in iambic pentameter, punctuated by perky rhymed couplets that utilize anapestic and dactylic qualities conjoined with clever use of slant rhyme.

This poem eschews sentimentalism. I do not intend to be sentimental toward my father, as he never showed the slightest sentiment toward me, though now and then he did command me to ride my little bike to the general store and acquire a carton of cigarettes or a flagon of whiskey for him, a gesture which, though fraught with illegality and smacking of apathy toward the sensibilities of a seven-year-old, still contained something of a loving symbiosis, the likes of which I will always cherish, not to mention it paved the way for me to start smoking and drinking whiskey at a tender age, which of course did not turn out to be wise or particularly healthy choices and which to this day I regret with all my heart and soul.

This poem is also a love letter to my tiny stuffed elephant, Bruno, who looms as a major figure in my young life. I have known Bruno since I could remember. He is blue and very soft and he jingles ever so sweetly. O Bruno, the things you and I have seen. Together Bruno and I milked the cows, fed the chickens, and watched re-runs of the Ed Sullivan show. Bruno is still with me, though he is so threadbare I was finally forced to have him sewn into the lining of my winter coat. Bruno, this poem is as much for you as it is for my dear father. Bruno, in so many ways you *are* my dear father.

This poem is an elegy of sorts, but it also uses some of the formal constraints of the limerick. Sort of an elegiac limerick, as it were, with playful rhyming but dour and dismal themes.

This poem uses constant alliteration. The letter "s" is featured prominently at the beginning and end of every line, as are the combined consonant sounds "ch" and "gl."

This poem came to me in a sudden, brilliant burst of imagination, and yet it has taken nearly two decades to draft. Coaxing the words from my brain has been like pulling toenails with pliers. I took out a second mortgage on my house in order to finish this poem. I had to travel to Greece, Italy, Spain, and New Jersey to study the necessary archival material in order to finish this poem. I had to become an expert swimmer, a champion ice skater, and a persistent phone solicitor in order to gain the kinds of experience necessary to write a poem of this quality and merit.

And now, without further ado, I would like to read you this poem.

# A Short Scatological Work

I shat and I shat and I felt satisfied
I shat until neighbors complained 'bout the flies

My wife and my family asked me to pack
I shat and I shat and I never looked back

I shat out my ass and I shat out my mouth
My poop became language in spite of itself

I shat out my eyes and I shat out my nose
The other locations I will not disclose

My poop was the subject of constant debate
Some thought it offensive, some thought it first-rate

I shat not for glory, I shat not for fame
Not money, nor power, nor pride was my aim

I shat for the little man making ends meet
I shat for the pimp and I shat for the priest

I shat on the hills and I shat on the plains
Though everyone begged me I would not refrain

My poop was the subject of news magazines
My poop was adored by both adults and teens

I shat through the night and I shat until dawn
The septic tank burst and it ruined the lawn

I was convinced that my poop would go far
The arc of my poop found its way to the stars

So proud of my poop as it shot into space
I shat on behalf of the whole human race

I shat out hard pieces, I also shat mush
I shat in a way that made everyone blush

I shat for my friend and he seemed rather pleased
He said he enjoyed my prolific feces

I asked him to join me and so we agreed
I shat on the floor and he followed my lead

According to what archaeologists found
In ancient times people just shat on the ground

# My Mortality

I felt my mortality today
in the cigarettes and eggs. In the seat
where I sit from morning till night.
In the friend I once held while he shivered and wept.

There! In the face of my ailing grandmother. In the
photographs of my dead cat!

My mortality in the piles of books I have barely read. In the dough
I knead till it tires my aching
shoulders and bones.

There! My mortality! In the family fruit basket, in each
suave and sagging diverticula, reddened and threatening
to inflame.

# Yearbook Quotes

"Simultaneously sympathetic and statutory"

"Bruised by ambition"

"Relate the straight fate"

"Happenstance happens"

"Shit shits"

"Clamp mammaries"

"Live-in nightmare"

"Boost the goose"

"Pilgrim mishap"

"Kill before mating"

"Wring the blood"

"The study of steam"

"Call up the cleaners, I pooped my outfit"

"Regular movements"

"Getting some skin removed"

"Stepping on saxophones"

"Shepherds on methadone"

# When I Used To Work at My Job

When I used to work at my job, I would get out of bed at 6am, make the coffee, feed the cat, eat an English muffin, take a shower, and leave the house by 6:45. I didn't have to start work until 9am, but I liked to arrive a couple of hours early.

My job mainly consisted of folding and bending. Sometimes I would collate. Every once in awhile I would be asked to apply the glue and seal the edges. This was the least pleasant job of all. Company masks, which were supposed to be made available at all times, were often not stocked, and I'd have to apply and seal with no protection at all. My eyes watered and my nostrils burned. No one else seemed bothered by this. My boss, who had hairy arms, was especially unsympathetic. And I found it peculiar that a man with such incredibly hairy arms would insist on rolling up his sleeves in every possible situation. Each morning I watched him arrive at the office in a two-piece suit. He would hang his suit jacket on a hook on the back of his door, roll up his sleeves past the elbows, and begin his work day. Just like that.

Most days, I could reasonably expect to fold and bend. Materials were left in my cubicle each morning, and I found that, with a two-hour head-start, I could be done with the day's work by 3pm. This meant that I had time to meditate in my cubicle for two hours before quitting time. Though I disliked my job, I did enjoy the meditation time. The hum of the machines downstairs blended in my mind with the smell of hot glue and the faint buzz of the fluorescent lamps. As long as we folded and bent our quota, and remained quiet and calm, we were free to do whatever we liked in our cubicles. I felt that the afternoons were entirely mine, and the fact that I was trapped in the office made it feel even more liberating somehow. Since my job required no communication, I didn't have a phone at my desk. No one could reach me. As far as anyone in the outside world was concerned, I was busy at work.

I read once about a man who practiced Kundalini yogic meditation. He woke up each morning at 4am and sat in the dark with his legs crossed. He concentrated on the image of a lotus flower. He meditated like this for years before he was finally rewarded with a vision. One morning he saw a brilliant, flashing fountain of stardust and electricity in his mind. Then he felt a burning sensation in his spine, starting from the nape of his neck and working its way down to his tail bone. The serpent that had been lying dormant at the base of his spine had finally uncoiled. His brain flooded with light and his body seized up on him. The experience was so overwhelming that he was unable to walk or eat solid food for weeks. He was fired from his job, and he nearly lost his family. He had no choice but to live the life of an ascetic monk from that day forward.

I meditated in my cubicle for two hours each weekday afternoon for nearly a year, but I was never able to achieve what the Kundalini man did. Once, though, when I had been applying and sealing all day without a mask, I felt dizzy and then had a vision of a diamond-studded glue gun floating in a glittery rainbow that arched above a massive sleeping elephant with multiple hairy arms. I woke up in the hospital that evening, and I quit my job the next day.

# Whole Note

Wait through measure after measure of rest until
one beat on the triangle rings loud,
wetting the breath-crowded air
with rivulets of silver-shaped aftertones.

Terrific backbone shaker,
maker of sweet, melodic honey drip.

Fruitful adventure vender, monotone bone toaster
laid to fester west of Hester Prynne,
tin man making saxophone heart pumps in cans of cat food
served in hard lumps.

We ran inside faster than advanced raster blaster
bounced bendable flippers expendable trippers
flaking mind matter bit by bit scattered eclipse
unfolding beneath moon-shaped step.
Great Waldo Pepper fending off relentless feckless navigators,
reminding mindless haters to mind their
famous manners.

# Amnihook

water breaking from big bubble
dispenser weighs in on anti-gravity amusement
park proposal and effectively stops discussion

due to serendipitous backlash maneuvering
learned from tower mamma lurking in cold alleys
always dominating subconscious and thus shaping

urban planning policy in
ways never before imagined
except in primal wombscapes or with pigeon duck

beach scenes lapping up brown water and wearing
holes in knees of jeans not sexual
but dirty in pancake underwear and yellowing photographs

boxed and stored under
cabinet stairs in stellar arrangement
bat fly hand dry blood stain on the kitchen floor

pie mat destroyed
mother skills wasted on lazy life hating
turkey basters who complain

they cannot access the pants

of ants and shy away from one-on-one

interjection favoring instead


cartoon representation

of self-mutilated

generation.

# Inside

We stay inside.

Inside our everything we talk about memory. We lapse
into questions. We look on the bright side.
If wisdom comes with age and anthropologists study the way we
    increase,
        we must then measure our everything.

We stay inside
and become westerly. We feel
there's no purpose for old people anymore.
And the world stays changing.

We crawl inside our rigid skins,
blanket the care,
hand-cup the ones we lean on,
and seize on the children of man.

Inside, I light the warm orange of these four walls.

.

# Stiff

## I.

I figured out what bothers me about Cleveland. It's the way he walks. He doesn't move his arms. It's disconcerting to watch a man stroll about with his arms held rigid at his sides.

## 2.

Sheila broke down crying at the pet store today. There weren't any customers around. She told me her brother had been arrested and then taken to the mental asylum. "This isn't the first time, either," she said. She looked so defeated. She has short dark hair and she wears a lot of make-up, so when she cried her face was a real mess. I told her I thought what she was going through was a real drag, and she said I was sweet. I wondered why she confided in me.

## 3.

One morning my hair was so frizzy and embarrassing that I couldn't go out all day. The next day, my hair relaxed. I walked down to the barber and told him to cut it off. The barber was a short man with a great big bald spot. He asked me why I wanted my hair cut. I was a little surprised that he would ask that. I said I needed to get rid of my hair so it wouldn't act up and prevent me from going places. He said he'd cut it, but he seemed reluctant. About half-way through the haircut, he just stopped, stood up straight, walked over to the counter, and started leafing through his schedule book, looking at all his appointments for the week. He murmured to himself, "Wednesday—Audrey, Chuck, Tom. Thursday—Michelle, Vincent. Friday—Annette, Bob, Scott, Milton." He looked at the schedule book and spoke to himself for a good three minutes before I felt I had to say something.

"You cut women's hair in here?"

He looked up at me. "Yeah. I start each day with a girl." He walked back and finished cutting my hair.

It was a great haircut.


## 4.

The café I usually stop at on my way home from work was closed. I mean permanently closed. It looked as if there had never been a business there in the first place. The windows were covered with paper, and the paper looked like it had been there for years. I knocked on the glass door. I waited for a moment and then heard voices. I looked through a tear in the paper, and I saw two little men crouched behind a big cardboard box. They were dressed in green. They looked like happy little men, and they were hiding. I knocked again and they just vanished. The box vanished, too.


## 5.

Cleveland knocked on my door today, but I didn't answer. He knocked and waited, knocked and waited, and then he peeked into my window. Was that necessary? He didn't see me inside because I keep it dark. Finally he walked away, his arms held rigid at his sides.

## 6.

I called Sheila and asked her if she'd like to come over. I said that I had been thinking about her brother, and she said I was sweet. She agreed to come over, so I got out my cologne and really covered myself with it. I waited for an hour. She never arrived.

## 7.

One cold evening I walked past the pink Victorian house that reminds me of my old aunt. She never lived in a house like that, but my aunt is warm and soft. The house isn't warm and soft, but still it reminds me of her. As I walked by, I heard "Amazing Grace" coming from somewhere within. I couldn't tell whether it was people inside singing along with a piano, or a recording of people singing along with a piano. I couldn't tell which would be nicer to imagine. I listened as I walked by, and I hummed to myself. It faded out as I got more and more distant from the house, and this, too, reminded me of my old aunt, though she is by no means distant, nor faded.

## 8.

I saw my barber in the check-out line at the grocery store. I didn't know his name, but I wanted to be friendly. I waved and said, "Hi." He looked straight at me and smiled, but he didn't nod or wave or anything. I kept walking. When I looked back he was still smiling at me, and the cashier was trying to get his attention.

## 9.

Cleveland came over to my place for dinner tonight. I sautéed collard greens and made some brown rice and beans. I'm not a vegetarian, but I never eat meat. Cleveland loved the food, and when he finished eating he was upset that there wasn't more. For dessert I made a peach custard pie. Cleveland told me over coffee that he was starting a band. He said he met a "chick" and that she was "really hot." After flirting with her for a while, he learned that she played the bass guitar and that she was looking for some musicians to start a group called "Strict Rigid Japanese Custom." She had the whole thing pretty well planned out, and Cleveland thought it sounded great. I asked Cleveland if she was Japanese, and he said he didn't know.

## 10.

I worked with Sheila today at the pet store and I asked her why she never came to my place after she said she would. She gave me a look that was supposed to be obvious, but I didn't understand. Instead of pursuing it further, I asked how her brother was doing. She smiled. "I don't have a brother, okay?" Then she told me I was sweet again. I asked her if she'd go out to dinner with me. She said she would think about it.

## 11.

Cleveland told me "Strict Rigid Japanese Custom" would play its first show in about a week. I couldn't believe how quickly they had come together.

## 12.

The café I usually stop at was demolished. I mean it was totally gone, not a trace of the little building that housed it. And there was already grass growing in the empty lot. I paused and stared at the space for awhile. A little man materialized. He sat on a cardboard box and held his arm out straight, as if he were roasting a marshmallow over a fire. I waved and made a clicking noise with my tongue, but the little man never looked up from what he was doing. I wasn't surprised.

## 13.

Sheila agreed to meet me at the "Strict Rigid Japanese Custom" concert. She smiled when I asked her and said I was sweet. To me, this felt like a real date. Before the concert, I rubbed myself with cologne. I used cover-stick to hide any blemishes I could find on my body. I wore the stiffest shirt I could find.

## 14.

After an hour I gave up waiting for Sheila and just walked into the club. It was midnight. "Strict Rigid Japanese Custom" were scheduled to start their set any moment. I walked past the bar and across the dance floor where ten or twelve people stood sipping drinks. I could hear a low hum and an electrical buzz. On stage, three people dressed in silver jackets and leather boots clustered around a fourth person. I walked closer to the stage and saw that it was Cleveland they were gathered around. Everyone had guitars strapped to them, including Cleveland, but Cleveland looked worried. I couldn't tell if the other band members were Japanese or not. They were touching Cleveland's arms and asking him questions. The electrical noise popped and crackled. Cleveland shook his head and strained his face. He looked like he was about to cry. One of the band members grabbed Cleveland's hand and made a chopping motion at his elbow. Cleveland looked down at his boots. After a few minutes, one of the band members approached the microphone and said, "His arms are too stiff. We can't play." The electrical buzzing stopped and some house music came blaring through the speakers.

## On a Serious Note

With vodka we bloat

Cigarettes and canker

We throw in the anchor

Pill popping, sliding down

Tubes in the warm wet

Creation and swimming pools

And glad mastication

We wake up all shit-smeared

And only want coffee

This cruel celebration

This giant fink nation

# Poetry Doesn't Need You

Poetry doesn't need you to dress all in black, to shave your head
bald, or to polish your boots.

Poetry doesn't need you to track all the times you've had dinner
with Ginsberg or channeled Rimbaud.

Poetry doesn't need you to lift it up out of some half-perceived
stupor or to rage at the youth whose attention you've lost.

Poetry doesn't need you to jump out a window or to burn your
lungs smoking or to carve up your skin.

Poetry doesn't need you to coax out its meanings or to tease out its
strategies or to unpack its bags.

Poetry doesn't need you to pinch yourself, wind yourself, catch
yourself spinning in spontaneous whorls.

Poetry doesn't need you to put forth sarcastic, bombastic,
gymnastic, fantastic ekphrasis.

Poetry doesn't need you to emulate or imitate its grandest
achievements or its infamous botches.

Poetry doesn't need you to wind it up, set it down, launch it or light it or warm up its hands.

Poetry doesn't need you to flirt with its dactyls or stroke its sestinas or unzip its pantoums.

Poetry doesn't need you to vibrate or widen your mindscope or suckle your cowsack or snuff up your hornblow or sweat out your insides or dredge up your backwash or kick in your facecloth or chisel your eyeteeth or sink into quicksand.

What poetry needs is a drink and a nap, and for all of its dinner guests—sipping on wine and straining their mandibles—to finally choke on the bones in their throats.

And what poetry wants more than any one thing is a volume of poems that nobody wrote.